the loose end
of the night

haiku

Paul Grant

First published 2006 by IRON Press
5 Marden Terrace, Cullercoats,
North Shields, Northumberland
NE30 4PD, England
tel/fax: +44 (0) 191 253 1901
email: ironpress@blueyonder.co.uk
www.ironpress.co.uk

ISBN 0-9552450-0-1

© Paul Grant 2006

Typeset in Garamond

Printed by Tyneside Free Press,
Charlotte Square, Newcastle upon Tyne

IRON Press is a member of Independent Northern Publishers

IRON Press books are distributed by Central Books
and represented by Inpress Ltd, Northumberland House,
11 The Pavement, Pope's Lane, Ealing, London W5 4NG
Tel: +44 (0)20 8832 7464
Fax: +44 (0)20 8832 7465
email: stephanie@inpressbooks.co.uk
www.inpressbooks.co.uk

for Laurence and Ellie

Acknowledgements

Thank you to everyone at IRON Press,
friends, family, the fine folk at
Monkey Kettle and Fortissimo Records.

Special thanks to Ruth
for all the support.

Photo: Stuart Southwell

PAUL GRANT
lives and works in
Milton Keynes.
This is his
first book.

start
continue
end

leaving for work
my sleeping cat
on permanent holiday

january snow
caught in the streetlights
breath

half open curtain
reveals
an empty street

a Sunday worth keeping—
coffee, toast,
eggs and sun

thinking less of you
the days
still full

the sit up machine
collects dust
as I eat chocolate

online with millions
feeling
disconnected

pylons cutting through the summer air
keep the sky
from falling down

the loose end of the night

this July evening
has me
staring down the sun

nothing to do
still can't find the time
to cut my toenails

trying on your glasses—
the world
bends

summer—
my cat hasn't moved
for six hours

downstairs moving out
their life
in boxes

my thoughts only go as far
as the end
of this pen

tv has me
dreaming
in commercials

different girl
same
mistakes

car horn—
not knowing who it is
I wave a hand

still star-gazing
groping
for something bigger

the photos finally developed
I see you
one last time

arriving at work
still dressed
in dreams

the loose end of the night

black bananas
white oranges—
time to buy more fruit

washing yesterday's face
down
the sink

in the distance
a lorry
shouts its name

as the train breaks down
a hundred people
take out a hundred mobiles

the same sunset
in
a different city

25 today—
my life
still on one hand

the loose end of the night

the evening cranefly
dances
into death's web

friday night—
chinese food
and tv reruns

while you discuss literature
I picture you
naked

today was
the size
of my eye

waiting for a call
... ...
still waiting

discussions on the size of the universe
from the world's smallest
bedroom

the empty page
at least now
a little full

while at work
my mind is as clear
as the floor I mop

boredom
the hours
like stone

every night
she sets sail
through my dreams

november fifth
the sky full
of crackling spiders

another day
spent waiting
for another day

the loose end of the night

an army of little green men
keeping the roads
safe

morning cough—
the countryside
calling

three birds
fly behind the building—
four return

when you left
you took everything
but me

on the radio
the music
comes with perfect static

starting the day
as I mean to continue
in bed

through my dirty window
I watch the window cleaner
across the street

winter—
your words
in little clouds

the city—
a duckling by day
a swan at night

will this torch
that I carry
ever go out?

dreaming dreams
of oceans
on my pillow

watching the sky
all thoughts
turn blue

the loose end of the night

standing in one queue
a woman
eyes the other

in the library
the sound
of privacy

at the wedding
my white shirt
turned pink by a red sock

sitting
at the crowded table
feeling lonely

rainy grey day
a crimson leaf
warms the pavement

deep winter
and death is hiding
in the old man's wristwatch

the loose end of the night

waking at 2:27 pm
the day
already spent

in the cinema
waiting for some action
so I can fart

this country life is not for me
my shoes
are set in concrete

summer moonlight
frames
your empty pillow

is the two o'clock bus late
or
is the half two bus early?

as she talks
I watch her lips
wondering where they've been

how lucky
the plastic couple on the cake
are

in the mirror
she creates beauty
for me to undo

spring breeze—
pink snow
falls

making a circle
I fit the moon
into my hands

my cat also can't sleep
and together
we watch late night tv

stepping on a snail—
the sound
of regret

sunday stroll
the pavement
dotted with gum

bread
ham
bread

is today's clock
a little louder
than yesterday's?

I go to say something deep
then
forget what it was

the girls in town
wear a rose
upon each cheek

monday afternoon
spent watching extinction
in technicolor

running out of poems—
another leaf
falls

arriving late
greeted by
an empty bench

as I return home
fresh milk
on the doorstep

under golden streetlights
even winter's bitter breath
is filled with beauty

as we talk
the candles
burn down

this haiku
interrupted
by your call

as I pass the mirror
I see
my father

december sex—
our socks
stay on

waiting
with hot steam and a spider
for the bath to run

too tired to write
anything
but this

weak tea
and rain
on a grey day

before going out
I rehearse my smile
in the bathroom mirror

the loose end of the night

on the men's room wall
a few names
of people in love

driving home
the streetlights
in full bloom

evening rain—
the clapping
of small hands

lip-syncing
the friday night
commercials

the date over
I place her
under the mattress

birthday blues—
more years
fewer presents

the loose end of the night

stack of letters
my name
absent

crushed box
reads
    handle with care

looking at the photo
trying
to remember the whole picture

"you're always so quiet"
she says
I don't answer

lost in thought
until the microwave
pings

finding a fresh patch of snow
I engrave
your name

do not eat the cake
says the note
on the empty plate

I turn on the tv—
another day
wasted

rough day—
my eyes
as black as iron

couples either side of me
my lips
unloved

standing up too fast—
snow
fills my eyes

with the subway train
comes the warm smell
of something

the loose end of the night

two joggers
trying to
outrun death

april sun
makes shadows
of everything

at the table
five friends
all talking into their mobiles

hours into days
days into weeks
weeks into years

watching her sleep
hoping for some small part
in her dreams

the leaf beside my feet
is also
far from home

the loose end of the night

at the traffic lights
a hundred strangers
waiting together

through our kiss
I taste the cigarettes
you claimed to quit

sunday afternoon—
rain, roast something
more rain

these weeks of boredom
have to add up
to something

trying to decide
which face
to wear today

riding the swings
my two cousins, come
closer and further away

my heart healed
I brave love
one more time

she dances in the mirror
so she never has
to dance alone

the glass is half empty
my life
is half full

ocean wave
breaks apart
against my leg

as it rains
a fire engine
rolls past

shot of wind—
the trees' leaves
come undone

christmas—
house lit
in electric snowmen

boxing day—
my belt hanging
by the last rung

you're wrong
but I want your lips
so I nod my head

quick!
my pen is almost out
of in

gang of teenagers
trying hard
to not try

after the fight
all my things
by the door

the loose end of the night

I want to go out
the moth
wants to come in

same thought
since you started talking—
brush your teeth

the party
at full swing—
I'm bored

smiles and handshakes
hide
our dislike

bowl full
of white, bruised fruit
crisp packets beside the bin

in your sunglasses
I talk
to myself

thick night fog—
the streetlights
singing quietly

with each drink
your lips
get bigger

still trying
to fit the world
into three lines

IRON Press is the UK's main independent haiku publisher. Try some of our other titles (add £1 per title for p&p). Our address is on page two.

Circling the Sunset
Maurice Tasnier
£6.00 ISBN 0 906228 59 X
Maurice Tasnier's highly original haiku are located in places such as doctors' waiting rooms, or draughty churches, as well as the form's more traditional natural world settings. Sometimes the short poems are sexy, sometimes humorous, and always observant, further emphasising how far the haiku form has developed over recent years in the UK. The author, who lives in Somerset, has won several awards, and his haiku have been translated into seven languages.

The Katsura Tree
Doreen King
£6.00 ISBN 0 906228 95 6
Doreen King is a distinctive new talent in English poetry; In this haiku collection her voice echoes through air, through wind and sea to oriental shores, capturing awareness island to island. The poetry links zen calmness with freshness and versatility. Frustration, despair, anger, joy and pain are all part of a life, and that life a part of nature, as the many conflicting moods and images are captured in this vivid collection.